USE OF INFORMATION COMMUNICATION TECHNOLOGY (ICT) AND DIGITAL INITIATIVES IN MODERN EDUCATION SYSTEM

RITURAJ BASUMATARY | DANSWRANG BASUMATARY

Contents

Abstract

The term ICT stands for Information Communication Technology. ICT is widespread and essential to play a meaningful and significant role in changing and modernizing the educational systems as well as the way of learning in this age of Globalisation in the 21st century. ICT is a part of many aspects of our daily lives today. ICT refers to the kind of technology which access to information. ICT includes any product that will store, restore, operate or receive information in a digital form. ICT is similar to IT that ICT focus more on communication which includes the things like the internet, wireless network and other communication mediums. There are some examples of ICT tools such as computing industry, telecommunications and electronic display.

Keywords:- Information, Communication, Technology.

Methodology

The methodology is adopted according to the need and objective of the study. The study is based mainly on secondary data collection. No sources of primary data has been used or collected.

CHAPTER I

Introduction

Technology has made it obligatory for people around the world to change the way they perform a task. ICT has become imperative for people bring changes in their methodologies in accordance with the technological advancement. ICT stands for Information and Communication Technology. It is an amazing changing power in the 21st century's age of Globalisation. Integration of ICT has enhanced the development speed in the entire education system as well as the works in our daily lives. Many such initiatives are taken to integrate it in learning and teaching process. In this age of Globalisation in the era of the 21st century, technology has made our lives easier and faster. Because of Globalisation today, we are living in a global village. Everyone is a Global Citizen today because of Globalisation. Technology has brought the distant places of the world closer to one another. Now a days, we can connect to each and every people living in any part of the world easily with the help of Internet. Technology has made the lives of people faster and easier. In the present scenario, no part of the globe is living in isolation but each and every part of the world are very well connected to each other. With the help of Internet, one can do many useful things like reading books, magazines, newspapers and journals in an online mode. We can also watch news, play and listen to music and songs by sitting in any place. Technology has made Globalisation more and more faster. Advancement in the field of Globalisation is mainly due to the advancement in the field of Science and Technology.

Because of Globalisation, we are able to live in an interconnected world where the seven sizes of the globe are very well connected to one another.

Now a days, we can do many things by sitting at our home itself. We can participate in different online events like seminars, conferences, workshops, meetings and so on.

CHAPTER II

Role of ICT in modern educational institutions in the present scenario in 21st century

Educational institutions like schools, colleges and universities started seeing integration of Information and Communication Technology in education as a thoughtful and a systematic approach towards assessing the entire process of designing, learning, utilizing, evaluating, developing and managing the instructional strategies. The use of ICT is highly significant in the fields of problem solving, comprehension, mathematical layout and composition that will endure learning as well as effective functioning throughout the life.

Information and Communication Technology comprise of a wide array of roles in education. Some of them being learning tools, communication, information sources, administration as well as distance learning. The "National Curriculum" requires students to be taught in learning computer from a very young age. So, as students' progress to secondary and higher level of education, they can easily adept themselves in using applications software. Due to this reason, ICT can be used virtually all the different subjects that are commonly taught to students. This includes English, mathematics, foreign languages, etc.

CHAPTER III

History, Origin, Development and Evolution of ICT in the period of modern education

In the 1980's, Britishers introduced Personal Computer's or PC's in schools and educational institutions. As there wasn't adequate amount of investment, each and every school was provided with just a single computer only. Most of the schools didn't even use them because the teachers weren't highly qualified and trained to deal with it. During that time, only a single Computer can be found in most of the schools.

CHAPTER IV

Advantages

ICT offers a wide range of services for the improvement of teaching and learning. Some of them being:

- Interactive and exciting teaching packages that are used widely on multimedia. These are DVD ROM's and CD that provides information in an attractive and innovative ways.
- offers quick and convenient access to information that wasn't available beforehand.
- It helps in linking schools on an international level.

CHAPTER V

Features

Some of the valuable features of ICT that assist in improving education standards are as follows:

- Internet service and tools,
- Distance Learning,
- Presentation Software.

CHAPTER VI

Relevance and Significance of ICT in modern education system

ICT is an essential and a widespread means to perform meaningful task in modifying and modernizing the present educational systems as well as the mode of learning. Not just education, it is a valuable part of several aspects of our daily lives in this age of the 21st century.

ICT is basically a technology that helps to obtain access to information. This technology includes products that will restore, store, receive or operate information in a digitalized format. This technology aims on communication aspect that includes wireless network, internet and other different forms of communication systems. There are several examples of Information and communication technology. A few of them being computing industry, electronic display and telecommunications.

ICT in the field of education is broadly classified in the form of a tool that aids in computer - based learning, research and presentation. ICT serves as an administrative tool that is useful in management of information systems. ICT not just has a great influence on education, schools and practitioners.

When talking about education, the objective of ICT is to acclimatize teachers and students with the right use of computers, with respect to its working and ethical as well as social issues. It is also believed that ICT empowers teachers as well as learners. It not just transforms the mode of teaching, but the entire learning process too. This transformation results in maximizing learning gains that helps learners to boost their creativity, communication and analytical skills.

Though ICT is highly useful for the entire society, it is seen to be more advantageous for school, college and university students. A learning experience rich in ICT help students to develop their ICT skills. With the necessary hardware and software provided to students, they can access all the needed knowledge from ICT. In this way implementation of ICT makes an educational institution smart, faster and progressive.

Compared to earlier period, with the availability of computers in schools, colleges and universities, students can carry out research quickly and finish off their assignments and projects much before the stipulated timeframe. This saves them a lot of time and increase their knowledge in using the machines. With ICT, use of machines and methods to acquire information from it becomes easy. Information and communication technology offer a wide range of effective lessons and information. Use of word processing aids students to perform their assignments easily. It makes their projects and assignments presentable, clean and organized.

This technology provides them access to abundance of information in a matter of seconds. It is found to be one of the best ways to improve their grammar and vocabulary skills. When learning in groups using ICT, students can benefit by collaborative learning. ICT supports local requirements for the learners that implies that social information can easily be found.

ICT infuses interest in students and make them participate more in the process of learning. Integration of information and communication technology in classrooms equips students with an ability to learn effectively, collaborate and explore the entire world around them. Anywhere and anytime access to extensive web-based tools encourages their learning not just within the classroom but beyond it too.

CHAPTER VII

Uses of ICT in our Life

ICT stands for Information and Communication Technology. The term refers to technologies that provide access to information through telecommunications. These technologies include the internet, wireless networks, cell phones and other communication media like radio, television, etc. By dint of ICT people are now living in an inter-connected world. We cannot think of modern life without ICT.

CHAPTER VIII

ICT in communication

ICT has created a 'global village'. Now, we can communicate with others across the world like next-door neighbors. Now, we have technologies like instant messaging, voice-over IP (VOIP) and video-conferencing. Besides, we have social networking sites like Facebook, YouTube and Twitter. All these allow us to remain in contact all over the world.

CHAPTER IX

ICT in education

The modern education system has become greatly dependent on ICT. Now educational institutions have multimedia classrooms. Students get computer and internet facilities. So, they can gather available information on their project or topic. Through the internet, they are also able to connect with the world-famous libraries for reading materials.

CHAPTER X

ICT in business

ICT has been a catalyst in modern business. Computer and internet technology enables companies to communicate with their clients, suppliers and distributors easily. So, businessmen can get information in time and can conduct their business successfully. E-commerce is flourishing all over the world due to internet technology. Various business organizations use ICT to advertise their products and services, hire employees and manage their business efficiently.

CHAPTER XI

ICT in modern banking

The modern banking system is the contribution of ICT. Today people can draw and deposit cash without going to the bank. They can purchase goods through credit cards or debit cards provided by the banks. They can pay different bills through mobile banking. Transferring money at home and abroad is now a matter of pressing a button on a mobile phone or a computer.

CHAPTER XII

ICT in medical science

Medical science is moving forward with the help of ICT. Now computers are used to diagnose diseases and make critical surgical operations. Internet, mobile phone, etc have facilitated the communications between doctors and doctors as well as between doctors and patients. Healthcare services have improved a lot due to communication technologies.

CHAPTER XIII

ICT in entertainment

ICT has brought a revolutionary change in people's recreational activities. Today people can have a lot of entertainment from mobile phones, television, computers, etc. They can find their area of interest and spend their pastime sitting anywhere.

CHAPTER XIV

Abuses

There is no denying the fact that ICT suffers from some abuses. Some people use the internet to bully and intimidate others. This is called Cyberbullying. Cybercrime or the use of computers in criminal activities has also become very common. Hacking and malware or computer virus are making troubles for many sectors. On the other hand, using ICT too much leads teenagers to addiction, isolation and passivity (OT).

CHAPTER XV

The Role of ICT

ICT is changing people lives everywhere. This goes from the home to the office. No matter who the person is they will have come into contact with ICT and it will have helped them in some way.

ICT has a big impact on people in their everyday lives and is affecting people in different ways. Technology is all around us but most people do not realise. It is taken for granted because of how common it is. The way it is changing people lives is though things such as the internet and mobile phones. Most people now have access to the internet whether it is at home or in the local Library. It is allowing people to find whatever information they want whenever they need it. We can also talk to people all over the world for free through instant messenger programs and Email. Mobile phones are allowing us to communicate at anytime anywhere we are. This means that people no longer have to either look for a phone box or have to wait until they get home to talk to someone. We can now phone people wherever we are even if on the other side of the country. We can just pick up a mobile phone and talk. This is making life better for people because before this technology people couldn't keep in touch easily and it could cost quite a lot of money to do so. Now we can communicate where ever we are. The bad points about this technology are the fact that people who do not have access are left out. Also this technology can be expensive and for some people it can be quite hard to learn how to use and so they are left behind and some people like the old ways.

Another disadvantage is people hacking and theft. Because of mobile phone there are more people being mugged in the street for their phone.

CHAPTER XVI

Conclusion

In this age of the 21st century as well as in the era of Globalisation, the use of ICT has become relevant. ICT is used in many disciplines be it Public Administration, Business Administration, Education and so on. It has made our works easier and faster. One can learn about the different events going on in the world simply by switching to the Internet. ICT has given a lot of welfare services to the people.

In today's interconnected world, information and communication technology (ICT) is widely used by our nation and it affects our lives everyday. It gives great impact in education for the learners and teachers. ICT has become a key driver in education way as well as it has been identified by a range of important wider benefits of ICT on learning. The positive impact of ICT on students' skills and teamwork are included.

ICT also help student and teacher with activities that are provided in the websites. That kind of activities gives ideas to the teachers in their teaching, so that students enjoy the class. Students learn more independently at the same time. They will take more responsibility for learning process. As seen from the information above, ICT can benefit both strong and weak students with their special needs. By the way, they especially improved the performance in student's English and on writing skills.

ICT is a part of a social system integrating meaningful communication within an education system. We can use it for analyzing the processes, meanings and functions of

ICT in education. ICT also provided the research for us when we have to do the assignments. ICT is also one of the tools that have easy communication with others in foreign countries. It saves cost and time.

Schools use ICT to make it easy for both students and teachers of their work. Different information and opinion can be found from the web-sites. In addition, ICT provides wide array of information and effective lessons. That is also easy for students to do their work by using word processing. It makes our projects or assignments more neat and tidy. From the education system point of view, "e" could mean "enhanced" education rather than "electronic" education. Consequently, ICT has a great impact on society especially on education.

On the other hand, ICT also has a bad impact on education system. Teacher who always show the example of the work from the internet and copy the information will not show a good example for the students. That may cause the students follow the action of the teacher and start to copy and paste. At the same time, the information and knowledge which come from the internet are not necessary correct. We have to be more careful when doing research from the web.

Moreover, it will cause the effect on the students. Students may not be interested in the way teachers teach. They will more focus on the web such as Facebook, MSN and Twitter. It unknowingly influences their result in the class. It also changes their behavior to the teachers in school.

Students who generally communicate with friends by the ICT will cause a problem when communicating face to face. It not only has an impact on character but also their attitude. Somehow, they will become more rebellious when influenced by the negative material. Today, we can see that have many teenagers use two or three phones. It will cause them not to pay attention in the lesson time.

In conclusion, ICT can give both advantages and disadvantages to education. We have to be careful when using it. Internet, TV, radio and others are the ICT that provide the news and information to us. We can increase our vision when we have it. But, when we are too focused on these things, we may suffer health problems by using them. We have to be wise in using the tools of ICT.

We cannot think of modern life without ICT. At the same time, we cannot deny the abuses of ICT. So, we need to be careful to ensure the proper use of information and communication technologies.

References

German, Tracey; Karagiannis, Emmanuel (2018). "Introduction". The Ukrainian Crisis: The Role of, and Implications for, Sub-State and Non-State Actors. Routledge. ISBN9781351737920.

Higgins, Andrew; Kramer, Andrew E. (18 April 2014). "Pro-Russian Insurgents Balk at Terms of Pact in Ukraine". The New York Times. Retrieved 7 April 2018.

Tsvetkova, Maria (10 May 2015). "Special Report: Russian soldiers quit over Ukraine". Reuters. Retrieved 7 April 2018.

Iulian Chifu; OazuNantoi; OleksandrSushko (2009). "Russia–Georgia War of August 2008: Ukrainian Approach" (PDF). The Russian Georgian War: A trilateral cognitive institutional approach of the crisis decision-making process. Bucharest: EdituraCurteaVeche. p. 181. ISBN978-973-1983-19-6. Retrieved 21 February 2016.

"Istanbul Document 1999". Organization for Security and Co-operation in Europe. 19 November 1999. Retrieved 21 July 2015.

www.ingramcontent.com/pod-product-compliance
Ingram Content Group UK Ltd.
Pitfield, Milton Keynes, MK11 3LW, UK
UKHW040014200726
13854UKWH00001B/196

9 798887 832852